In His Time

Reflections on Walking with the Lord

Jan Truesdale

Scripture quotations are from The Holy Bible, English Standard Version (ESV), copyright © 2001 by Crossway Bibles, a publishing ministry of Good News Publishers. Used by permission. All rights reserved.

Copyright © 2016 Jan Truesdale

All rights reserved.

ISBN-13: 978-0692708088 (JT)

ISBN-10: 0692708081

A Note from the Author

As I look back over my life thus far, as the writer of Ecclesiastes says – there are many seasons. There have been times of sorrow and times of joy; times of despair and times of hope. The underlying girder is what holds each of us during the roller coaster of life. That girder is, of course, our heavenly Father, Almighty God.

As you read through these poems, if, at times, you feel that the sentiment is too discouraging or barren, I encourage you to turn ahead a few pages to a season of hope and joy. All of these emotions fill these pages as I reflect on my journey with the Lord.

A Time for Everything

3 For everything there is a season, and a time for every matter under heaven:

[2] a time to be born, and a time to die;
a time to plant, and a time to pluck up what is planted;
[3] a time to kill, and a time to heal;
a time to break down, and a time to build up;
[4] a time to weep, and a time to laugh;
a time to mourn, and a time to dance;
[5] a time to cast away stones, and a time to gather stones together;
a time to embrace, and a time to refrain from embracing;
[6] a time to seek, and a time to lose;
a time to keep, and a time to cast away;
[7] a time to tear, and a time to sew;
a time to keep silence, and a time to speak;
[8] a time to love, and a time to hate;
a time for war, and a time for peace.

Ecclesiastes 3:1-8

God created seasons. Life <u>is</u> change. Each season has its unique challenges as well as blessings. Going through the various seasons will hopefully draw us ever closer to the Father. Even in times that feel challenging, Our Lord is there; and in times of blessings, hopefully, we feel His presence. But one thing is consistent -- change is an integral part of our lives.

As I have experienced many changes in my life, I have often been drawn to reflect upon the change and the circumstances of my life. As I look back over this, I can see the hand of The Lord at work, even in those times when I was not aware that He was there.

A Psalm

Alleluia!
The Lord is here!

I feel His presence
In a love so real
It is almost palpable.

I celebrate the sweet mystery of the Holy Eucharist
As once again
My Father lovingly offers me Himself.

I see Him
In majestic, towering trees –
Zig-zag branches silhouetted against the blue-gray backdrop of
    evening skies.
He speaks to me
In the stillness.
The scent of wet leaves after this storm
Offers me His aroma.

The very air is full of His presence.
I breathe deeply;
The Holy Spirit replenishes me,
Pervading my innermost being.

All senses rejoice
In the presence of the Lord.

A Wild Rose

The climbing rose was wild,
Untamed,
Untended.

Tendrils wandered off randomly in all directions.
Dead branches mingled with the live,
Abrupt interruptions to its potential beauty.
A few blooms dared erupt from time to time,
Their sparseness marking a distinct contrast to the whole.

One day the Master Gardener came in;
He clipped and pruned.
Fallen branches cluttered the ground.
The vine cried out in protest and anguish.
But He offered water,
Fed the little plant, and gently encouraged its growth.

Soon – new flowers appeared,
New leaves,
Even entire new branches adding strength to the creation.
The bush took on a very pleasing shape as
It produced perfect white roses
For its covering.

All who saw it were amazed.

Waves

Waves gently lapping at the shore,
The rhythm soothing and calming.

Then a sudden, unexpected shift of the wind,
A thunderous crashing as the relentless waves beat in
One after the other.
No rhythm -- only loud crashing,
Unyielding, unmerciful pounding of the surf.

The memories come crashing in one after the other,
Overwhelming.
I am drowning in the sea of remembrance.

Coming in too quickly to assimilate,
Too harsh to endure.

Whimpering,
I race for the safety of the dunes,
The protection of distance.
I gasp for breath
As I run for shelter.

But reality ...
No lifeguards on duty tonight,
No safety nets in sight.
Only barren dunes --
Sand dune after sand dune
In endless procession,
Like the monotony of loneliness
With no oasis on the horizon.

Only endless waves
Crashing in one after the other.
Will it ever end???

What a Year!

What a relief!
It's hard to believe this nightmare year is finally over.
(Except for those last few loose ends).
It is good that
We do not have the power to see into the future,
Because if I had known
What this year would bring
Maybe
I would have been tempted
To say
Deal me out this time;
I'll pass.

Yet that would have been a mistake,
Because
While this has been the worst year of my life,
In many ways
It has also been one of the best.
The confusion and doubts
Have been dispelled
And replaced by
A new awareness—
Of myself and what it is I really want from life.

The price was high,
But the lesson is invaluable,
And I am a better
(and much happier)
Person now than I was a year ago.
When my whole world first began its slow, agonizing destruction.

I wouldn't want to relive this year,
But I'm glad it happened.

And perhaps
There was no other way.
Perhaps
The unpleasantness has to be experienced
In order to be able to
Fully appreciate
The difference.

From this is coming
A new beginning,
And how many people have such an opportunity?
I must be careful
To utilize this opportunity to its fullest.
Make the most of it
And the new optimism which it brings.

Real People Sometimes Live in Magic Places

Some recognize only reality;
Some reject reality for magic.
A few understand
The intertwining relationship of magic and reality.
They rearrange reality at will,
Dissolving barriers between what is
And what we want it to be.
Sometimes magic is,
And sometimes it is created.

Reality changes with our expectations.
Expectations can create magic.
Can you rearrange reality?
Can we take what is
And make it into what we want it to be?

How we look at life
Is what creates the magic.

Does magic exist?
Or must it be created?

Making Omelets

Can you make an omelet without breaking eggs?

I tried to put all my eggs into one basket,
But the basket wasn't completed
So the eggs began to tumble out.
Gently I caught them
And frantically began to juggle
Lest one should accidentally be broken.

I can't make a new basket
With my hands full of eggs.

So I'll just lay them on the shelf in the meanwhile.

From Regret to Joy

Regrets?
That it took me thirty-two years to understand what I need to learn.

Sorrow?
For those people who never realize it

Joy?
The realization of who I am
And the slowly-dawning comprehension of who I want to be.

Sea Gulls and Solitude

It's eight o'clock on a cold Sunday March morning,
The park peopled only with silent, cool monuments.
Empty benches await those who will come later,
Now occupied by shafts of brilliant sunlight reflected off the gray water.
The sea gulls are a row of plump, fluffy statues along the rail,
Briefly still, then once again soaring through the sky –
Now gliding,
Now diving toward the vast grayness in search of food.

The blue of the sky begins to appear as the wispy white clouds drift toward the horizon.
In the distance a plane speeds through the sky,
Its course straight and true, never faltering, never wavering
As the sea gulls swoop and soar underneath.

A group of young men approach;
Their thin jackets a poor protection against the sharp breeze.
Greasy hair sticking to necks,
Their identity coming from their sameness.
Furtively, I glance around,
My serenity interrupted by this alien intrusion.
A flicker of suspicion interrupts my thoughts,
But they continue down the sidewalk,
Only briefly glancing my way,
Nonchalantly dismissing my presence.

Across the water, the shore seems quiet, serene, undisturbed.
Yet in those homes (which appear to be only a row of doll houses)
There live real people.
Even now they are filled with the sounds of living;
Sounds which remain unheard on this far shore.

Peace? Calm??

The house is so quiet that
I can hear the birds singing outside.
A warm feeling of contentment is present,
A calm interlude before the demands of the day.

The sound of the approaching blue behemoths
Shatters the peace
As I begin the mad scramble
In the usual Friday race.
The men in the dusty orange overalls
Love to smile triumphantly when they win the race.
They enjoy watching my mad dash to the curb
Only to arrive there just as they pull off.

But today is different.
I am victorious.
But I do not stay to savor the victory –
I return
To try to recapture that feeling of
Peace and calm.
It isn't the same though.
Those demands have begun
And are becoming more insistent as the sounds of the clanking
      garbage cans
Awaken the children
With their demands for attention.

What Once Was

Emptiness!
A feeling of being totally alone –
My heart feels icy;
I gasp for breath.
A gray, bleak mist settles in.
My foundations crumble underneath me;
Frantically, I grasp for support
And find –
NOTHING.

Desperate now,
I accept the reality of this hell
And the totality of the emptiness.
I am
Anguished
Bereft,
ALONE.

Land of Folly

A wisdom ancient as the ages
And as new as that first tender bud of spring.

Once upon a time
A very long time ago
(Or was it really yesterday?)
A very special place came to be.
The Land of Folly
Is a magical, mystical place.
No shoulds or oughts fill its essence,
Only golden dreams and visions.
It never rains
(Unless you love rain).
The flowers are always in bloom
(Until you want autumn's bright palette).
And sharp icy snow appears with a thought.

The Land of Folly
Is founded on a wisdom ancient as the ages
Yet is as new as the first tender bud of spring.
Its inhabitants have a rare ability
To rearrange reality,
Dissolving barriers between what is
And what we want it to be.
Sometimes magic is,
And sometimes it is created.

The Land of Folly
Is a real place,
But you can't get there by car
Or plane or boat.

No horse or camel knows the way.
You must find your own way there

For the Land of Folly
Exists within the human soul.
Some reject reality for magic
And recognize only wizards
And dream of magic wands and Aladdin's lamp.
Some only know reality;
They scorn what they cannot explain.

Only a few understand the intertwining relationship of reality and
    magic.
Only a few can conjure up fairies
And find their way to the Land of Folly.
For to reach it
We must look within our own hearts.
We must allow our dreams and private wishes
To take command
Of our souls.
We must be able to hear the piper
And dance along behind.

The Land of Folly
Is never the same place twice.
Like quicksilver, it flows through our imagination;
Its boundaries changing as quickly as they are established.

We <u>ARE</u> the Land of Folly
We inhabit it and contain it within us all at once;
We each create
Our own Camelot.

PROMISES

A meteor shower - -
My mind's eye
Immediately conjured up
A scene of dazzling beauty
As stars exploded
In a brilliant display of nature's finest fireworks.

Two shooting stars
(I was promised hundreds)
Evaporated
In the rosy glow of dawn.
The brightly twinkling heavens
Fading into gray even as I watched.

Promises are so often like that.

Expectations
Crumble and wither,
The brightness merely an illusion
Against the dull grayness of reality.

I Don't Know Who I Am Anymore

I feel my self-confidence seeping out.
It escapes
A little at a time
In faint wisps of smoke,
Dissipated,
Gone.
Leaving vacant spaces.

My assurance withers
And begins to disappear;
Only a hard shriveled knot remains,
Barely recognizable.

My inner strength
Erodes,
Crumbles away;
Leaving small heaps of dust.

My spirit needs shoring up;
My soul cries for encouragement.
I search for comfort,
And find –
Emptiness.

Walls

With temerity
And trepidation
I exposed those inner thoughts,
And looked around,
Feeling rather foolish
To discover my vulnerability.

Then –
The defensive walls
(Outside my volition)
Went up
INSTANTLY!

Now I must begin
The slow, laborious task
Of tearing them down.
Perhaps you will help
By occasionally gouging out
A brick or two here and there.

Love

I have a whole lifetime of love stored up.
It wells up within me
And refuses to be contained.
It flows over
And spills out –
Sometimes inopportunely,
Always spontaneously.
Often I find myself
Alone.
Love can be so overwhelming
That it drives others away.

The Singles Scene

They seemed so desperate
Yet so self-righteous.
They go out to meet people
Yet withdraw from real contact.
The thought of being alone
Seems terrifying,
Yet they are afraid to reach out.

The laughter is shrill, high-pitched –
"Notice me, everyone."
Yet echoes falsely.
It is underlined not with mirth or true enjoyment
But a false hope
That laughing will
In itself make one happy.
"See me – Isn't this fun?"

But the desperation never quite disappears.
They hover in groups,
Afraid of being alone
For fear someone will consider them rejected.
The conversation
Always returns to
That lowest of the low – the ex
And contains various profound comments
About how rough life is
And aren't they coping well?
"Look at me – Haven't I adjusted beautifully?"

And they continue the desperate search
For they know not what;
Perhaps they will never find it.

What Do You Do When You're Tired of the Noise and the Crowds?

The metrical, musical clinking of the halyards
Punctuates the darkness
In the womb of the boat.
The monotonous motion mimics the gentle swell of the waves,
Slowly lulling me to sleep
In this refuge from reality.

I experience an interval of peacefulness,
As I set the world aside
For a brief slice of time
And create an ephemeral respite
Of quiet calm and tranquility.

Empty Heart

Is it all right to feel lonely?
Is it okay to be scared?
If I say it out loud,
Will it go away?
Or get worse?
How do I comfort myself?
Silly, meaningless rituals
Offer only the illusion of comfort.
Is there anyone
Somewhere
Who really cares?

There's an empty spot in my heart,
In my life;
And it cries to be filled.

Longing Heart

Lonely means crying for help
And no one hears.
Lonely is a heart filled with longing
And no one cares.
Lonely means when the load becomes too heavy to bear alone,
No one is there with a helping hand.
Lonely means needing a hug
But none are available.
Lonely is bleak.

Loneliness

Loneliness
Is not the same thing as being alone.
Alone can be good:
Independence leading to
Self-confidence.
Loneliness creeps up from behind,
(it can even strike when you're surrounded by people).

Sometimes
I need to know I'm not totally alone.
I need to know that someone cares if I'm frightened.
Sometimes
I need reassurance.
I need someone who will listen to my fears
Without laughing and with understanding.

Sometimes I need to voice my feelings
Because confronting fears and worries
Is never as frightening as trying to pretend they aren't there.
Loneliness is despised
Yet accepted as part of the price for alone.

An Encounter

Wandering
Through the events of my life,
Confused, lonely, and (I have to admit it) more than a little
 frightened,
When I had an encounter –
A simple encounter.
Seemingly
An ordinary meeting
With an ordinary man.
Yet it became something more:
An encounter with my God.

Not such a simple event after all.

The man perhaps didn't realize or understand.
But I knew,
And so did God.

Where do I get a Second Opinion?

How do I find God's plan?

Is it like looking for a new outfit?

Do I keep trying them on
One after the other
Until I find one that fits?

And do I accept my judgement?
Or do I ask for a second opinion?

Is the color right?
Or would the other one be better?
Do I keep trying them on for size --
One after the other
Leaving behind the discards
In tired little heaps?

How do I find the one God has for me?

The Father's Voice

Tired of running in circles;
I collapse in my resting place.
Where is my direction?
My purpose?
My passion?

I hear the Father
Calling me;
Telling me to look only at Him.

Calling me to prayer.

As I quiet my spirit
And tune out the noise of the world,
His voice
Becomes clear.

He offers me whispers of His love and guidance,
Filling me with His peace.

As I rest in Him
I am overcome by His love;
I fall asleep in the midst of offering thanks.

I awake to a new sense of purpose as I seek to follow His leading
And hear His gentle whisper as I go through my day.
No more confusion;
No more worry;

Only a deep peace,
A peace that passes all understanding.

Thank you, Father.

Friends

Will you be my friend?
Will you hold my hand when I am scared?
Will you laugh with me when I'm happy?
Will you hold me close and stand by me even when I'm not very
 lovable?
Will you share my triumphs and comfort me in my defeats?
Will you accept me as I am – enjoy my strengths and endure my
 weaknesses?

If you will be my friend …
I promise you total loyalty.
I promise you to always be there whenever you need a friend.
I promise you I will still be your friend even in those rare moments
 when I might not even like you.
I promise you more care and concern that you ever expected.

I need a friend;
Do you?

Child's Play

The child in me
Wants to come out to play.
She was lost for a while;
But just yesterday
Her smile peeked around the corner of my heart,
As her laughter
Echoed joyfully in my spirit.

Frustration

Here it is
Three years later;
And an old frustration resurfaces.
Expectations can create chasms
Where secret caves
Hide disappointments.

A Three Act Play

The ocean
Offered its customary tranquility,
Jangled nerves quietly sighed
As calm was restored
To inner circuits,
And tension
(The unwelcome intruder)
Fled before the advancing waves.

The movie theatre
Offered a new setting
For ever-increasing awareness.
Holding hands
In silent communication, we forged a link
Like co-conspirators
Against reality.

The park bench
Offered a welcome retreat
As conversation became more intense,
And we began the requisite ritual
Of subtle explorations
And the very gradual
Lowering of masks.

Friendship

An unusual and somewhat unorthodox beginning.
Sometimes our trek through life
Is interrupted by a brief detour to smell the daisies.

Close friendships don't always come easily
But once formed, they are nearly indestructible.

Building a friendship
Must be like building a house.
We begin with the foundation:
Mutual trust and respect.
Depth comes with each shared experience.

Tired

I have others fooled
But I can't fool myself.
I want to lean on someone
(Only briefly – for renewed strength)
But the only one I can rely on is
Myself,
And I am so tired.

Help

I need some help.
I don't know where to turn,
Or whom to ask;
I'm not even certain what the question is.

Cleaning House

I couldn't discard my faith
So I put it on the shelf –
Way in the back,
Behind all the boxes.
I took it down occasionally,
Dusted it off,
Tried it on, briefly enjoyed its warmth, and then
As the dark voice whispered false encouragement,
I once again shoved it into the hidden recesses of the clutter and
 confusion.

Until …
One day
I had an encounter with my Lord –
A life-changing encounter.
Together
God and I brushed off the cobwebs
And renewed the shine.
He wrapped my faith around me
And gave me enough love
To begin the laborious task
Of cleaning out the debris.

Anger

The anger is so large
It steals my wind,
Leaving me breathless
And becalmed in a swirling maelstrom of emotion.

I feel powerless and insignificant
In the face of such gargantuan feelings.
The explosion, coming as it did
With no prior rumblings,
Astonished me and ignited internal flash fires
Which fed off each other through the interminable night.

Where is Calm?

Anger is my enemy.
It takes my strength from me.
Afraid, speechless with a nameless fear
I flee
To that safe haven deep within my soul
Where only God's angels can follow.

An Evening at the Ocean

The waves rolling in
One after the other
Continuous,
The same, yet ever-changing.
The continuity lulls my mind;
The magnitude reminds me of my own insignificance.

As the daylight fades,
First the moon appears, a shining half orb surrounded by a hazy
    glow,
Next the first star twinkles brightly,
As we each make a private wish.
I wonder if we ever outgrow all our childhood beliefs.
The magic is not as strong as it once was,
But I am reluctant to disavow it completely
(Just in case).

Soon the water is only a silver-gray form in the darkening evening,
And it becomes impossible to distinguish one wave from another.

But the sounds remain.
Soothing, peaceful.
I reach out;
Our hands touch.

The Trap

Dependency is a trap.
Trust me (they say);
Rely on me.
The bait is alluring –
A sense of security,
A relief from worrisome pressures,
Promises of hopes being fulfilled.

Wary at first,
Uneasy.
But soon reassured by words;
Lured in by dreams,
I begin to succumb and believe.
Tentative trust works its subtle hold.
I become courageous,
Confident,
Even daring to trust the words and promises
Believing this time will be different.
When –

SNAP!
The trap is sprung.
Why do I always take the bait?

Hurt

Hurt so unbearable
That it must be walled off.

Hurt
Looms larger,
Threatening my very existence.
I wall it off.

Anger

Angry with God?

Awesome

If he were a vengeful God,
Would he strike me down for my audacity?
Throw a burning bush in front of me
To stop my brazen behavior?

But no, He is loving.

He is my Father who loves me dearly and calls me to be His child.

Waiting

Why is waiting so hard?
Why do I always want to know the outcome quickly?
Am I being impatient?
I know God has only my best interest at heart in His plan.

Why is the unknown so frustrating?
It's God's plan
In God's time.
Is it fear of the unknown?
Am I reluctant to put it all into God's hands?

Wait on the Lord
Sounds so easy and simple.
Putting it into action
Not such an easy task.
Lord, I want to move forward;
I want to plan.
What is this waiting all about?

You know the end from the beginning.
Why won't You show me?

Patience?
I didn't know that was part of the deal.
I can depend on You,
But I want to see some action.

Lord, you are good
Your plans are always what is best for me.
Help me lean on You during this time.
You are my rock!
Your outcome will be pleasing!

Business as Usual

The Lord spoke to us.
First he told us to pray.
He lovingly repeated the message in various forms until
Eventually we "got it."
Great and mighty plans were laid -
Much scurrying about to and fro.
At last the great day arrived!
We met together for a vigil, and
No surprise!
The Lord showed up.
Not only that, but he once again spoke - loudly and clearly.
Specific instructions were given to various pray-ers.
He spoke in a still small voice heard by everyone.
He told us to change our ways;
He told us that it was not to be business as usual at our church.

Oh, we were properly grateful, praised and thanked Him for
    revealing Himself to us,
Then we patted ourselves on the back
"Good job."   "Well done."

Excitement in the air;
But Satan did what he does only too well,
As the excitement turned to pride and self-satisfaction.
"It is holiday season - must attend to all those details "
Special services, different schedules.
Not even slowly, but almost all at once
Our busyness began to replace our business with the Lord.

What was that He told us?
Oh we compiled a beautiful report.
What a job!
Nicely done, neat and easy to read.
Good job. Well done, as we once again congratulated ourselves on
    doing the Lord's work
After all, He really wants those special services at Christmas;
He wants all of us to come together to celebrate Christmas.

Surely He didn't mean Christmas when He said it was not to be business as usual

All too soon, the holiday season was history,
The packed services a memory.
Worship?
Some did.
Others "did church."
Were lives changed?
Well, we don't know;
We were awfully busy, Lord, doing your work.

Our Lord has infinite patience.
Again He told us
It is not to be business as usual.
But Lord, we must find new staff, and church elections are so time consuming.
"Not business as usual"
But Lord, we'll get around to reading and trying to interpret what you meant;
We just have this church business to complete first.

Not business as usual

But Lord we always do these things - every year.
And this year is especially difficult with things being in a state of change around here.
The Lord sighed, and He spoke once more.
"When will you children learn?"
"What must I do to get your attention?" He pleads.

He is still infinitely patient, but time somehow seems to be running out.
It's still business as usual around here.
Nothing much has changed.

God spoke.
People faithfully recorded His words,
Then went about their business as usual.

The Piano

Each time my fingers
Meet the keys,
I am overwhelmed
By the thought
That someone once loved me enough
To give me the gift of music,
And that he understands
My need to create
In order to be fulfilled.

In times of despair
I retreat into that world of total concentration,
Finding hope for an interval.

Chaos to Calm

My eyes on my circumstances –
    Outcome: confusion
My eyes on Him, my Comforter –
    Outcome: Peace.
Release from the entangling circumstances.

Chaos turns into calm
As I focus
Only on the important:
My Savior
My Redeemer.

Wandering

I was wandering on the path of the expected,
Doing what was right in the eyes of others,
With little regard for what My Lord wanted from me.

What caused me to see The Light? What caused me to pause and
 look around?
No dramatic event;
No showy display of God's omnipotent power --
Just that gentle nudge, that softly whispered word
To bring me back to His way.

Jesus saw my pain;
He knew my uncertainty.

I was wandering,
I was confused
Seeking, Searching, Striving.

Til I found the answer.

Then I knew:
His way is the way;
His way brings me life;
His way brings me joy.

His way, His way is the ONLY way.

Alleluia I have found your way;
Alleluia I have found your peace;
Alleluia I have found your strength.

Alleluia I know You!

Rest for Moms

Peace.
Quiet.
At times so elusive,
The challenges create inner turmoil and steal your rest.

Yet the Lord always knows:
The job of Mom does not come with on/off buttons.
Just as the Lord has no on/off times.

Know that joy will always follow the frustrations
As the Holy Spirit fills you to overflowing.
That peace that passes all understanding
Will pervade your soul and spirit,
And overflow to that precious baby.

Rest in the Lord.

The Ocean

The ocean –
Ever mysterious,
Relentless,
Constantly moving,
Constantly changing
Yet unchanging.

The magnitude is awesome.
Humbling
Yet
Soothing,
Calming.

When I feel troubled,
Watching the infinite waves
Roll in – one behind the other,
Never-ending,
Calms my turbulent thoughts,
Eases the tension.

I need to go to the ocean tonight.

Self-Confidence

Give me confidence, Lord.
Not self-confidence (as the world sees it)
But God-confidence;
Strength from Your presence within me.
Help me march to a different drummer
As long as that drummer is You!

This is faith!

Come, Holy Spirit

Banish Satan and his minions from our hearts and lives.
Banish him now and forever.

Bring us your peace.
Let us come before you with praises and singing;
Let us proclaim your love to the world.
You are our hope and our salvation;
We will not fear as we walk beside you.
Guide our steps.

Thank you, Lord.
You are surely our hope in time of trouble,
Our threshold in time of fear.
You are our refuge and our strength.
Help us feel your presence always.

Lord, calm the troubled waters;
Command the waves to cease their turbulence;
Bring smooth sailing through the days ahead.
Be our guide;
Let us not speak in haste,
Nor run ahead of your leading.
Help us to feel your true peace.

Take our burdens, Lord.
Carry them.
They are so heavy.
We cannot do this alone;
We need you, Lord.
This is not possible without you every step of the way.
Keep us ever mindful of that,
And keep us aware of your presence always

Lord, stones and snares are ahead of us.
Show us how to navigate
And negotiate
The sharp twists and turns in the path.
Lend us your guiding light;
Go ever before us and smooth the way.
Make the crooked path straight
Just as you promised in your word.

Guitar Strings

After too many years of inattention
They were rough and coarse,
Frayed.
The notes sounded flat and dull,
Tired, worn out --
The songs not quite in perfect tune.

Then inspiration struck --
New strings!
Attaching them was a tedious, mundane task
No excitement, no laughter, no joy.

Tuning took some time,
Getting each detail just right.

At last!
The feel now smoother, easier.
The taut strings took on a life of their own.
The music exuded a scintillating sparkle;
Matching the twinkle in his eyes.

But ahhh . . .
The sound.
The melody brighter;
As the notes rang clear and crisp.

Fresh excitement filled his fingers and drifted up to his heart.

He wrote a new song.

Where Can I Go?

Where can I go?
Where can I turn?

Trouble is everywhere;
Darkness surrounds me.

But when I worship You, I see Your Light.

Lord, let me worship you and not grow weary.
Lord, turn my face to yours.
Lord, I love your peace.

When I forget and begin to wander,
Lord, draw me back to you.
Let me worship you and not grow weary;
Lord, turn my face to yours.
Lord, I love your peace.

Draw me ever closer;
Draw me back to you.
Let me worship and not grow weary.

Lord, turn my face to yours.
Fill me with Your peace;
Lord, fill me with Your peace.

Guide

It should be a simple journey;
I have the best guide
And the ultimate guidebook.
Yet the complexity of it
Has me completely baffled.
Where do I go for help?

Wisdom

How do I know God's will?
I am mere man
Clumsy, foolish, blundering.
Where do I find wisdom?
And how do I recognize it when I find it?

High Stakes Poker

I put all my cards on the table
But you weren't ready to play.
So I picked them up
And tucked them away
In an inside pocket
(the one next to my heart.)

Who has The Key?

We're on the same train,
But we have different timetables.
Attempting to coordinate our journey,
We become ensnarled in varying time zones.
Only the conductor can straighten out our confusion.

I withdraw behind that invisible protective shell,
Retreat back to firm ground and security;
Draw the curtains tight,
Bar all the doors;
Then wonder –
Did I leave the key in his pocket?

Gold

Is it like searching for gold?
Fool's gold
Glitters and gleams
Luring the unwary.
True gold does not sparkle
Until loving hands polish it.

Peace

Lord Jesus Christ
Let others see You in me.
Give me Your mind;
Let me have Your peace.

Lord Jesus Christ
Let all worry cease.
Give me your mind;
Let me have Your peace.

When worldly turmoil
Threatens to overcome;
When tranquility is but a fleeting thought,
And trouble makes me numb,

Lord Jesus Christ
Let me be least.
Give me Your mind
Give me Your peace.

Ash Wednesday

On my forehead I wear the outward mark of ash;
Take it inward, Lord.
Mark me as Your own.
Let my outward way
Reflect Your inward Light
So that
The world will know whose I am.

As we reflect on your ultimate gift to us on this holy day,
Let Your love fill my heart
And manifest itself in my daily thoughts and actions.

Lent

Ashes
Rubbed on my forehead --
A reminder of my mortality
And my sinful nature.

Yet …
The cross
A reminder of Jesus' immortality
And His forgiveness.

As I reflect on these things
I am overcome by the Father's love
As He calls me into a time
Of prayer and reflection
In preparation for the Easter celebration.

A Lenten Meditation

God woke me in the morning with a simple word:

"Pray."

His Spirit filled the room,

Lovely
Peaceful
Quiet:

"I walked with Abraham;
I will walk with you.
But you must make room for me beside you.
You must be quiet inside
So you can hear me,
And I will show you the way to go.
I will put happiness in your heart
Which will be reflected by the smile on your face.

You are mine.
I love you,
I will take care of you.
I will give you your innermost desires!
I placed those desires there to begin with
So you will want what I want for you.

You are my child;
I will care for you.
Put your hand in mine
And walk with me.
The journey will be exciting,
Yet peaceful.

Tell me your troubles;
Do not hide them from me.
I am God;
I am all-powerful.
I can ease your troubles;
Do you doubt me?
Put me to the test.
Give up your worries;
Let me handle them.
I want to care for you just as you care for your children.

Surrender your willfulness,
And peace will surround you.
I will only show you a step at a time.
My total plan is overwhelming.

Trust me;
I will guide you.
Take the next step,
Then I will reveal the next one to you.
But each step of the journey
Will bring increased happiness
And peace
And joy of the heart,
The joy that comes from walking with me.

Do not be distracted;
Do not listen to other voices.

I am here;
I will not leave you.

Even when you cannot feel my presence,
I am there!

Have faith.

I led Abraham;
I will lead you.
I am a changeless God.
You read about me in my word.
I still have those same qualities.

Withdraw from the loud noise of living from time to time;
Come talk to me.
I am always ready to listen.
Keep your spirit calm and peaceful
So you can better hear my words.

Be still.
Be still.
Be still;
I will be there."

Thank you, Lord.

Lenten Reflections

Lent …
The call to give up focusing on life's unimportant details.

Shift my focus
From the unimportant
To the Only One who matters.

I kneel in reverence,
Thinking on the Father's faithfulness
And His unchanging character.

I am overcome with awe
As I meditate on His sacrifice
And His unfathomable love.

My prayers of petition
Turning into praise
As thanksgiving fills my heart.

Easter

Celebrate the risen Lord!

He is risen?
How can that be?
We just laid Him in the tomb,
Rolled that enormous rock in front,
Securing the tomb from errant invaders.

What do you mean?
Where is He?
You saw Him with those disciples??
Hallucination?
Wishful thinking?
How do I believe this?

Reality sets in
As I face the open tomb,
The stone rolled to one side.
Peering in, I see only a vast emptiness
As the truth overwhelms me.

He is risen!

He is risen indeed!

Easter Season

Do we celebrate only one day?
Or do we allow the excitement
To pervade our life?

If Christ is truly risen,
How can we celebrate one day,
And then return to the daily routine?

Life is now different
Because of what He has done for us.
Life will never be the same again.
This gift too large to totally comprehend.
I must take it in
In small pieces.
How could He love me that much?
Did He really rise?
Or is it just a myth?

Slowly
Realization settles in.
He truly loves me that much.
If he paid that price for me,
How do I respond?

He gave His life for me.
I must give my life to serving him
With joy
And anticipation
And overwhelming gratitude.

Ardor or Apathy

What is the best approach?
To life?
To work?
To play?

How do I approach each day?
Reluctantly, laboriously, doubting?

OR

Eager
Energetic
Excited

The writer of Proverbs spoke to this very issue.
His words are direct:
A little slumber or too much rest,
And poverty comes on you like a bandit,
Scarcity like an armed man.

Attitude determines actions.
My actions offering others a clear picture into my heart.
Spiritual apathy brings on spiritual poverty.

Once again Proverbs' wisdom:
Haughty eyes
A lying tongue
Hands that kill the innocent
A heart that loves evil
Feet that race to do wrong

A false witness who pours out lies
A person who sows discord among brothers.

These are all things that the Lord hates.

Reap what you sow.
Am I sowing good seeds?
Am I sowing seeds of ardor or an attitude of apathy?

A right heart and a right attitude.
How do I do that?
There is only one way:
I must be right with God.

Orphans No Longer

Once we were orphans.
Alone,
Walking in the dark
Danger luring us in.

Until
The ultimate sacrifice occurred;
An unfathomable love,
Overwhelming mercy.

Not earned
Or deserved,
But still our promise to claim.

Now we are sons and daughters of The Most High!

Perspective

Fixing my eyes on those charts
Reading line after line of random letters,
Attaining the best vision possible through lenses.

New glasses bring new clarity and sharpness to vision.

Then comes reflection:
Where am I focused?
Is my vision on physical things?
Or on spiritual things?

Where am I looking for guidance in life?
A person who is highly respected in the business world?
One who has attained great wealth?

What are my goals?
Worldly success?
Material possessions?
All can be good things,
But am I accepting the good instead of the best?
Am I looking at what I don't have?
Or am I focused on the good that I have?

Is my perspective temporal
Or eternal?

As I contemplate, I hear clearly:

Focus on the Lord;
Fix your eyes on Jesus;
Follow the Master.

Storms

Storms are a regular part of life
At times a rare occurrence,
Other times flashing with ferocious frequency.
Where do I focus during the storm?
Where is my attention?

My eyes blink at the brilliant flashes of light,
My hearing overwhelmed by the thunderous clamor.

Time stands still.

Until I seek His refuge.
Fix my eyes …
Not on the circumstances and conflict,
But on The One who can quiet any storm.

I only have to ask.

Our Time

There is a time for everything under the sun.
Will our time come?
That is yet to be seen.
For now, we will enjoy our "moment in the sun."
If this is to endure, only time will be the test.

As we learn each other in oh so many ways,
As we discover new delights,
While practicing patience.
The sweet pleasure of one,
The anticipation of the other,
Makes a delightful, yet exasperating experience.

This time of testing, trying, tantalizing --
Will it prove to be enduring?
Will it live up to promises?

The hope is true,
The wish sincere;
Yet, as always, time will surely tell.

Happy as A ...

Happy as a clam?
Really?
Hiding in the mud,
High tide bringing
Cover and
Anonymity.

Then –
Low tide
Brings exposure.
This happiness flees
As the hiding place is exposed.
Safety is no more
As clam diggers
Descend on the bed.
Nowhere to hide.

Sigh!
Then the waters roll in again.
High tide
Restores the place of safety and security.
Happy as a clam
At high tide.

Happy as a lark --
Singing as it soars
Through the sky.
The exhilaration of freedom and flight.
If larks could smile
He would wear a large grin at all times.

But
He continues singing
And soaring,
Always happy
Always singing.

Memories

Memories
Bits and pieces
Floating up to the surface of consciousness
Like dead fish
In a polluted pond.

Maps

Driving down the highway
I realize
I have misplaced my map.
Did I leave it at the last stop?
Should I go back and try to find it?
Or go ahead and look for a new map?

Cross Roads

It happens all too frequently
In the natural flow of life.
A cross road looms.

Bewildered
We stop,
Overcome by uncertainty.
Where do I turn?
Which way do I go?
Which one is the right path?

Fear is a growling lion,
Unbelief an insurmountable obstacle.
The voice of the evil one
Rings out clearly, yet with deceit:
Go my way.

As I stop and ponder,
Trying to ascertain my course of action;
I listen for the one true voice.

I look down the path ahead,
Asking where is God?
Which direction does He want for my life?
He longs to show me,
But the distractions draw my focus away from Him.

Fear paralyzes me
Until I spend time with the Father.
Then
Faith frees me.

I stop and listen,
Hearing the voice that I seek.
His direction is clear.
I move forward;
No looking back,
Walking in faith.
The only true way
Is His way.

Look Back or Go Forward?

Memories
The bitter
And the sweet
All mingled together.

Memories of other times,
Other people.
But that is all in the past.

I must look ahead,
Forget the past,
Bury it,
Be done with it.

Plans,
Hopes,
Desires for the future
Will only occur
When I live in the present.

Goals

When I pursue worldly goals,
I find a momentary and fleeting sense of satisfaction;
When I pursue God,
I find joy and peace.

When I look at the world,
I see chaos;
When I look at God,
 I see everlasting beauty and serenity.

When I occupy myself with temporal things,
I become self-focused;
When I occupy myself with God,
I become God-focused -- with a view of eternity that eclipses all
    else in this temporary life.

When I seek success and attain it,
I become haughty and self-dependent;
When I fall and look to God for help,
I become God-dependent and filled with true joy.

So where do I have my eyes? Where am I focused? From where
    do I draw my strength?

Only from YOU, oh Lord,
Only from You!

Demands

Sometimes the demands of life
Come rushing in
Demanding all my time,
Commanding all my attention.

Yet …
Where is the joy?
Peace is elusive.
The busyness a distraction.

I stop.
Retreat
To that secret place
Where peace abounds.

The Road to Maturity

Ministry growth
Often follows a pattern of human growth.
The infant stage --
Happy with little things;
Small rewards bring big smiles.
Content to let it happen.

Then comes childhood --
Curious,
Always seeking more.
Sometimes falling down or stumbling in eagerness,
But always continuing the quest.

Then, hang onto your hat!
As we enter
The turbulent teens.
Rebellion is rampant.
Chaos is the norm
As we seek maturity.
The learning process a challenge.
The reward of maturity well worth the work it requires.

Lord, guide us through the turbulence
Knowing Your peace awaits;
The joy of walking in *Your* will
In *Your* time!

Joie de Vivre

A joie de vivre
Exhibited
In your boundless energy and enthusiasm
Unequalled by few.
It contagiously spreads among those
Who have the privilege of knowing you.

Respect shown to others
Is returned to you
As you inspire us
To reach beyond ourselves
And teach us about life
Through your living of it.

A deep respect for others
Reflected back
As in a mirror.

Dedicated to a former mentor!

Fireworks

Dazzling flashes of poetry against the dark canvas of the evening
    sky.

Unexpected --
Breath-taking even,
But so quickly ended.

The oohs and aahs fizzle out with the last remnants of the lighted
    firmament.

What must it look like to God?

Is He amused by our silliness?
Is he laughing with us in our foolish attempts to separate light from
    darkness?

Childish glimpses of power that vanish as quickly as they appear.

No lingering to savor the memories;
Everyone quickly rushes to pack up and trek to the waiting cars.

Hurry home
Before the memories fade.

Mundane talk replaces the breath-taking sighs;
Headlights pierce the dark atmosphere
As we foolish creatures leave this brief glimpse of God's everyday
    display
Of stars and universes and galaxies.

And we never look back.

Forgiveness

How do I forgive one who has wronged me?
One who has hurt someone I love.
Forgive?
He doesn't deserve it;
He broke my loved one's heart.

Forgive him?
Really?
Why should I forgive him?
He is the one who did wrong.

Then I reflect on Jesus,
The price He paid.
Do I deserve His forgiveness?
Have I earned it?
Forgiveness is not earned
Nor is it deserved.

When I hold on to unforgiveness
Will God forgive me?
Or must I let go
In order to receive
His forgiveness and love?

As I reflect on these questions
He leads me to His word.

Ah –
The Father's prayer offers instruction.
He teaches me
To ask for His forgiveness
As I forgive others.

His forgiving me
Shows His love for me,
And shows me His desire
That I forgive others in the same way.

How do I do this?
In my own will and strength --
Impossible.

Walking in His will and
In His strength,
All things become possible.

Once again – I thank You, Lord.

By the Water

One lone duck floating in the vast expanse of the river;
Two tug boats heading toward the harbor,
Ready to accompany the next large container ship to its mooring.
Three church steeples loom above the horizon;
A myriad of boats of all kinds lazily rocking at their respective
    docks.

One lone sailboat at anchor, sails furled.
Two blackbirds eyeing each other with suspicion
As one quickly devours the stolen bait.
Three men fishing,
Eagerly awaiting the catch.
A myriad of folks stroll by, each intent on his particular
    destination.

One cruise ship at dock,
Anxiously blows its horn calling passengers aboard.
Two chimneys at the Cigar Factory
Standing tall and steadfast
Through all the changes at its foundation.
Three geese honking noisily as they fly by.
A myriad of sea gulls,
Each flying his own route, oblivious to others

Everywhere I Go, I See You

When skies are grey
Or when skies are bright and blue;
When all seems old
Or when all things are new;
Walking on the beach
Or sitting in that pew;
Toiling through ordinary
Or enjoying a majestic view.

Walking through life with My Lord --
Everywhere I go, I see You.

Regardless of circumstances or the place,
One thing is true:
Everywhere I go, I see You!

From Cocoon to Butterfly

Shoved into a cocoon (not of my own making)
A stifling confinement.
The illusion of safety brought a flicker of hope
Only to be extinguished as the
Darkness and despair became overwhelming.

Cocoons are confining and constricting,
The fit too tight.
Beating against the walls brought great weariness;
My eyes began to adapt to the dim light
And the lack of form or substance.

Then somehow, some way
A faint glimmer of light appeared;
Next, the outline of a distant horizon . . .

Was it possible?
I renewed my flailing;
The walls slowly fell away and
Crumbled into dust.

Were those wings?
Is that sunshine?

Then confirmation:
He said,
"You have butterflies in your eyes."

Floating Down the River

Floating down the river
Oblivious to my surroundings,
Enjoying the gentle rocking as I float.
Until
That sudden and abrupt halt.
Was it a dam?
Or a large boulder?
Blocking my progress.

Then a gentle transition
Into smoother waters,
No blocks in the way.

I ponder as I float on down the river,
And a voice whispers,
Welcome!
You have left the river of self.
Welcome to the river of God.

Life

One thing is consistent:
Everywhere I go, I see You!

Just another day in that endless stream of activity;
Busyness abounds.
Traffic irritates and annoys.
Then
I drive over that majestic bridge
And catch a glimpse of the beauty of the endless flowing water,
Birds soaring overhead.
You are there!

Sitting in the waiting room
Annoyed by the screaming baby;
Then
As I leave, encountering the engaging smile on the baby's face,
His countenance radiating the father's love.
You are there!

Sigh!
On to my next appointment
I arrive
Only to discover:
No nearby parking place.
As I walk to the building
A squirrel scampers through that tiny piece of refuge in
Trees lining the parking lot.
You are there!

I head home;
Evening chores and cooking await.
After dinner, relaxing on the patio
Seeking peace.
The breeze seems to carry off the stresses of the day
As I enjoy the sight of birds nesting in nearby trees.
You are there!

I reflect on the day, and
I see one thing clearly:
Everywhere I go, I see You!

Geese and Turtles

Placidly lazing around on the shore of the pond.
Enjoying a grand picnic

A gaggle of geese
All sizes.

A large family reunion?
Some resting lazily,
Others marching through the grass
One behind the other.
A few taking a leisurely stroll.
Some eating
Some napping.
Others wandering along the shore,
Occasionally stopping to peck in the grass
Then lifting that long neck to gaze around.

On the opposite shore,
A horde of turtles
Encamped in clusters of quiet shells.
Occasionally a head pops out,
Looks around,
And then retreats back into his place of safety.

Large turtles
Baby turtles
All oblivious to their surroundings.

Sea gulls soar by.
Then a sudden dive
Interrupts the placid atmosphere
Of relaxed geese snoozing in the shade.

Geese marching in tandem;
Do they hear a silent drummer?
Placed yet determined.
They stand up
Shake their feathers
Baby geese lying quietly in the shade
Observing all the surrounding activity.

Just another placid day as
God's creatures
Enjoy their existence.

Distractions

Focus?
Why is that so challenging?
I know what is important.
I know what is essential.

Yet
I still allow the distractions of this world to occupy my thoughts
And use my energy.

My focus becomes distorted.

What has my attention?
Where do I spend my energy?

Lord, call me closer to You
Draw me away from distractions

Armadillo

Being an armadillo comes with many advantages.
That rough rugged outer shell
Offering protection from life's hurts …
A safe hiding place.

Seemingly impenetrable,
Until another conceives a way to turn him over
Exposing his vulnerability.
The soft, tender underside facing upwards,
Unguarded
Unprotected
Open to hurt;
But also
Open to healing
As the raw spots are restored.

Rejuvenated,
He runs off once more,
That outer barrier
Firmly in place
Offering protection and safety.

River of God

River of self -- I drown
River of God -- I surrender control
The decision seems obvious.

Why do I find myself drowning?
Until I seek the true river,
That river of life
From which I receive all things good.

River of God – again

Flowing in the river of self,
Gasping for breath
As tumultuous waves wash over me.

A moment of respite,
Quickly followed by an endless line of overwhelming waves.
I lift my hands toward heaven
Pleading for deliverance and help.

The waters calm briefly
Allowing me to see a passage into new waters.

With trepidation I peer into this river.
Do I leave the known?
Venture into the unknown?
The rushing waters push me into that place of calm.
I relax and float in the River of God.

Sunday Saints, Monday Sinners

Sunday morning
Get up and go to church,
Feel righteous
Because I am doing the "right" thing.

Monday morning
Get up and go to work.
Do I really have to tell the truth all the time?
Sometimes a 'white lie" feels necessary to keep up appearances.

Sunday
Pray and talk sweetly to God.
Monday
Curse God or one of His children.

How am I to do this?
People might think I am strange
If I talk about God in the workplace.
Don't want to sully my reputation in the community
By being a "fanatic."
Someone might take offense
And take their business elsewhere.

How do I do this?
Only with the help of the Father.
I am a sinner
Redeemed only by the extreme love of the Father

Sunday Saint?
Yep, that's me.
Monday sinner?
Yes, but now a forgiven sinner.

Free of guilt,
Walking through my days
With the Holy Spirit by my side.

Joint heir with Jesus,
What a heady thought.
But this brings that ultimate responsibility.
No matter my earthly lot
I choose to stand with Jesus.
Live a life that is pleasing to the Father.
A life of gratitude
For God's goodness
In spite of Satan's futile efforts to destroy God's handiwork.

Monday sinner for sure,
But a changed, redeemed sinner.
I want the world to know
The source of my joy.
Lord, thank you for allowing me to live this abundant life,
Gratitude and servitude to the Father.

Pleasures of Life

It sounds so appealing --
Pleasure beckons.
Worldly desires.
Life will be perfect;
You only have to:
> Buy that
> Do this
> Go there.

Alluring . . .

Yet, the satisfaction
Is short-lived.
The experience dissipating into vapor
As disillusion sets in.

This life is fleeting;
Pleasure momentary;
Peace elusive.

I let go;
Stop chasing after rainbows and
Give up control
As I allow God to take the place of self.

Anxieties disappear;
The void filled to overflowing by the Holy Spirit.
His will for my life
Supersedes my wildest imagination.

Transformation
As thoughts become new;
His will supplanting mine.

How good and pleasing and perfect
Is His will for me.

I transition:
From pressure to peace
From worry to wonder
From self to Spirit.

Lighthouse

Standing in the shadows
Furtive
Hiding
Suspicious of those around me.
Blinders preventing me from seeing clearly.

Other people viewed with skepticism
Do they avoid me?
Overlook or ignore me?

A faint flicker of light --
Quickly hidden,
Yet never extinguished.

A candle allows sporadic glimpses
Into the darkness of the world;
Then a lamp
Shining brightly for a small radius,
Offers brief hope.

Finally
A lighthouse.
There is brightness all around me.
Others are drawn to the brightness
As God uses me to be a lighthouse
And ultimately a beacon.

Am I a lighthouse?
Does God shine through me?

Others drawn
Not to me,
But to the light that shines.
My spirit inhabited and
Taken over
By His brilliance.
His light
Shining truth to all who see it.

Attempt Great Things for God

Attempt great things for God.
What am I doing?
Is it great in the sight of the Lord?
Or merely humdrum, mediocre?

Where are my expectations?
If I always expect the same thing
That is what I will achieve.

Lord, help me set my sights higher in You.
Where do You want me to go?
What do You have for me?

When I attempt great things for you,
I expect great things from YOU,
As you are my hope;
My source of strength.
Guide me where You want me to be.
Give me peace in my heart
As I lean on Your strength
And not my own.

Timing

Life
Tide
Ebb and flood in intricate rhythm,
At times frothing and crashing in the power and fury of a storm,
Other times lazily lapping the earth's edge.

Now turbulent
Then tranquil,
Advance
Followed by retreat.

Ebb and flood –
Never-ceasing,
Often unfathomable.

Always awesome.

Hands

My hands outstretched to receive your blessings;
Your hands outstretched on the cross.

My hands reaching out to help a friend in need;
Your hands healing the whole world.

My hands raised in praise and adoration to You;
Your hands gently leading me on Your path.

The toddler's hands grasping the hands of his father as he takes
    those first wobbly steps;
The Father's hand offering security and sure footing.

My hands clasped as I come before you in prayer;
Your hands reaching down to receive my sacrifice of praise.

Reflections

Reflecting
On the good
And the not-so-good
Life has to offer.

Remembering
The events that caused me pain
And brought sorrow
As well as the ones that brought such great joy.

Renewing
Those promises I made at such a young age
When perhaps I didn't truly understand what life was all about
Or how God would direct my paths.

Results
Are overwhelming
As I consider
God's plan for my life
And how He has walked with me through the valleys
And the mountain tops.

Results that I could not have foreseen
All those years ago
When I first declared Him as my Lord and Savior.

Rejoicing in His love
And His mercy in my life!

ABOUT THE AUTHOR

Jan Truesdale has been writing all her life. Much of the writing was personal and only recently did she decide to compile some of her favorites into this book.

Her professional career includes high school English and Journalism teacher, broadcast sales and management, and professional coaching.

www.ingramcontent.com/pod-product-compliance
Lightning Source LLC
Chambersburg PA
CBHW032143040426
42449CB00005B/375